CARING FOR THE PLANET
DESERTS

Neil Champion

A+
Smart Apple Media

Published by Smart Apple Media
2140 Howard Drive West, North Mankato, MN 56003

Design and production by Helen James

Photographs by Getty Images (American Stock, SAMUEL ARANDA / AFP, Adrian Bailey / Aurora, Pierre Barbier / Roger Viollet, John Burcham, Robert Caputo / Aurora, Richard Dobson, Jason Edwards / National Geographic, George Grall / National Geographic, Katharina Hesse, Chris Johna / National Geographic, Mattias Klum / National Geographic, Frans Lemmens, Lisa Limer, James Marshall / Image Works / Time Life Pictures, David McNew, Marc Moritsch / National Geographic, David McNew, MPI, Carsten Peter / National Geographic, Joe Raedle, Joel Sartore / National Geographic, George Silk / Life Magazine / Time & Life Pictures, ESSAMAL-SUDANI / AFP, Selwyn Tait / Time Life Pictures, Medford Taylor / National Geographic, Roy Toft / National Geographic, Ann & Steve Toon);

Library of Congress Cataloging-in-Publication Data

Champion, Neil.
Deserts / by Neil Champion.
p. cm. — (Caring for the planet)
ISBN-13 : 978-1-58340-513-0
1. Deserts—Juvenile literature. 2. Endangered ecosystems—Juvenile literature.
I. Title. II. Series.

QH88.C39 2005
577.54—dc22   2004056458

First Edition

9 8 7 6 5 4 3 2 1

Contents

Earth is an amazing place. It is complex, beautiful, and awe-inspiring. There has been life on it for some three and a half billion years. In all that time, it has grown more complex as life-forms **evolved**. Today, there are more species of plants and animals—about 10 million according to one scientific estimate—and more **habitats** in which they live than at any point in Earth's long history. This is our inheritance. It is this that we are changing at a faster rate than ever before. Our ability to alter the environment to suit our own purposes has never been greater. This allows many of us to live longer, more active lives. These are positive things. However, there are sides to our development and expansion that are not so positive for the planet.

The Desert Biome

Environmental scientists divide the world up into large natural zones called biomes. These biomes include deserts, **temperate** woodlands, rain forests, **tundra**, grasslands or prairies, oceans, and rivers and wetlands. Each biome has a certain type of climate and is characterized by its plant and animal life, which is adapted to live in the conditions it offers.

This book looks at life in the desert biome and the threats deserts face today. It also looks at some solutions to these threats that may protect what is left of the natural world.

An Arid Environment

Scientists define a desert as an area that receives less than 10 inches (25 cm) of precipitation a year. Scientists also take into account the rate of **evaporation**, which has an impact on the available water. They divide dry environments into three types, depending on how arid, or dry, the land is. Very arid areas (true deserts) receive less than 4 inches (10 cm) of rainfall a year; arid areas get 4 to 10 inches (10–25 cm). Semiarid lands receive between 10 and 20 inches (25–50 cm) of rainfall a year.

It is often assumed that deserts can't sustain much life with such little water. While it is true that deserts are among the simplest **ecosystems**, and that their extreme dryness cannot sustain an abundance of life, it is not true that deserts are barren. They vary enormously and sustain a variety of life more plentiful than might be thought. In fact, deserts cover around one-third of Earth's surface and are home to more than 10 percent of humankind.

Deserts occur on every continent, although in Europe they result from **deforestation** and overgrazing, actions of people rather than nature. Today, deserts are increasing. This worries scientists, because although deserts are beautiful environments in their own right, there are plenty available naturally, and their increase is due to overexploitation of the land by people.

How Deserts Form

Deserts occur in nature due to very specific geographical circumstances. There are four main types of deserts. Tropical deserts form between latitudes of 5° and 30° north and south of the equator. In these regions, the air is warm and has little or no moisture in it. The deserts of Baja California and the interior of Mexico are examples of tropical deserts. Continental deserts are far from the seas and oceans, and therefore the land and the wind are very dry. Examples include the Gobi Desert and the Takla Makan, both found in the center of Asia. Rain shadow deserts occur on the dry side of mountain ranges. Clouds shed their precipitation as they rise over the mountains, leaving none for the land in the rain shadow. The Mojave and Sonoran Deserts lie in the rain shadow of the Sierra Nevadas. The Atacama in South America is another rain shadow desert. Coastal deserts are found where cold ocean currents create dry air masses. The Namib Desert in southwest Africa is an example of a coastal desert.

Highest Dunes

The Namib Desert in southwest Africa stretches for 1,000 miles (1,600 km) along the Atlantic coast. It contains the highest sand dunes in the world, some up to 1,000 feet (300 m) tall.

George Silk

How Hot Is Hot?

The hottest temperature ever officially recorded was 138 °F (59 °C) in the Sahara Desert in northern Libya in 1922. In California's Death Valley, summer temperatures can climb above 129 °F (54 °C). Temperatures are measured in the shade, since a person standing in the sun at these temperatures would risk death from severe dehydration. Deserts are also famous for their diurnal temperature range, the difference between the highest and lowest temperatures in one day, which can be as great as 54 °F (30 °C). The annual temperature range is also high, especially in continental deserts such as the Gobi in central Asia. Winter frosts are not uncommon in many deserts, including those in the southwestern United States.

Man-Made Deserts

Deserts around the world have both grown and shrunk due to the natural processes of geological and climate change over vast periods of time in Earth's long history. However, in more recent times, another agent of change has appeared—human civilizations. The ancient world is littered with lost cities that grew too large for the surrounding countryside to support their population. The soil became barren in trying to cope with the crops grown on it, and water sources dried up. The result was **desertification.** The process is still going on, and today it can be seen in parts of Spain, where deforestation and overgrazing have created barren, semiarid areas that are still expanding.

Striking Landforms and Desert Shapes

Hot deserts have more in common than just dryness. Strong winds, rare rainfall that typically occurs in heavy downpours, and hours of sunshine with hot daytime and cool nighttime temperatures all help shape desert environments. A lack of vegetation makes deserts vulnerable to erosion by wind, rain, or floodwaters. The shapes and colors of desert rock and soil are not covered or softened by plants, which gives deserts their uniquely stark appearance.

Hot and Cold Deserts

People generally associate deserts with heat. The Sahara and Australian Deserts are typical examples of hot deserts. Hot deserts do get cold, however. They often fall well below freezing at night because there is no cloud cover to keep the heat in. Temperatures in the Takla Makan and Gobi Deserts often drop below freezing, mostly at night. Even Antarctica is considered a desert. Although it is a land of snow, ice, and glaciers and is permanently frozen, it is classified as a desert because it gets very little precipitation.

Amazing Rocks

Striking rock formations at Red Rocks in the Mojave Desert. This high plateau landscape (up to 6,000 feet, or 2,000 m) of the southwestern United States sees a huge variation in daytime and nighttime temperatures, which leads to intensive weathering.

This bareness also makes deserts prone to weathering. Rocks are subjected to such high temperatures and wide temperature changes that they readily break up into smaller rocks and sand. In the winter and at high altitudes, frosts also shatter rocks. Chemical weathering occurs, too, when minerals in the rock are

Desert Sandstorms

A sandstorm moving across the dry landscape of Kalahari Gemsbok National Park in South Africa.

What Is a Sandstorm?

Deserts get lots of wind, caused by very hot temperatures near the ground. A lack of vegetation means there are no plants to slow these winds. In sandy areas, the wind can pick up sand and dust, creating a sandstorm that can travel great distances. Southern England occasionally receives red dust from the Sahara Desert in Africa, thousands of miles away.

broken down by rainwater or moisture in the air reacting with carbon dioxide to form a weak acid. Deserts have lots of mineral deposits because the rare rain that does fall washes minerals down from surrounding mountains. Wind plays a major part in desert erosion by sandblasting. It picks up sand and drives it against upright surfaces, wearing away soft rock layers and leaving harder ones, often forming striking shapes in the process. All of these processes also mean that deserts can feature amazing colors, whether from layers of bright-colored minerals that form surface varnishes, or from the exposure of different layers of rock.

Desert shapes include deep canyons, **mesas**, pillars, and arches formed through desert erosion. Mushroom blocks are formed when sand blasts a large rock, wearing down more of its lower section to give it a top-heavy, mushroom-like shape. Sand dunes are a prominent feature of some deserts. They are created when loose sand is blown by the wind and collects to form ridges. Sand dunes cover more than a quarter of the Sahara, the world's largest desert, and nearly 40 percent of Australia's deserts.

Where Does Desert Water Come From?

What little water deserts have is crucial to the life they support and critical in ensuring the survival of the biome. So where does this water come from? Rain is rare, typically falling as an isolated rainstorm. Much of it evaporates, some is used by plants and animals, and some runs into short-lived dry rivers or filters into aquifers below ground. Dry rivers, or wadis, flow after heavy rains and then dry up as the water evaporates and filters into the ground. Aquifers are underground layers of porous rock that hold water. Some are fed by rain; others are deeper and contain so-called fossil water that dates back thousands of years to before the area was desert. This water is not replenished, so although it can be drawn up with wells, it must be used carefully. Another water source in some deserts is meltwater from snow and ice on nearby mountains.

Some rivers are big enough to flow right through a desert, bringing water to strips of land along their banks. The Nile is a famous example. Since ancient times, this river has brought water and soil-enriching materials in the form of silt to the dry regions of Egypt from its mountain origins in Sudan and the Ethiopian Highlands far to the south. Another example is the Colorado River, which brings water from the Rocky Mountains into the deserts of the southwestern U.S. Traditionally, people living in desert regions used river water to **irrigate** the surrounding lands, but today, dams have created many artificial lakes and large-scale **hydroelectric plants**.

Desert Flowers

The smallest amount of water in a dry place will allow hardy plants to develop and flower. This plant is growing out of a sand dune in Australia.

Where Are Earth's Deserts?

Deserts are found all over the world, in a variety of different geographical regions—from low coastal plains to high mountain plateaus. As has been shown, there are various types of deserts, and there are many geographical and climatological reasons for why they exist where they do. The amount of degradation that occurs in any desert is often related to how close to centers of human habitation it is and what mineral wealth it offers. Remote deserts are usually safer from human interference than ones with large cities close by—unless they harbor something people value, usually in the form of minerals and precious and semiprecious stones.

North America

The North American deserts lie mostly in the southwestern U.S. and Mexico. They include the Great Basin Desert, the Mojave Desert, the Colorado Desert, the Sonoran (or Yuma) Desert, which straddles the U.S.-Mexico border, and the Chihuahuan Desert, largely in Mexico. There are smaller areas as well, such as Death Valley in California and Nevada. The Painted Desert lies in Arizona and is named after its bright bands of colored rock. The population of some of these areas is growing because many people are attracted to the stable and sunny climate. Water is a major issue, with high demands made on the Colorado River. On California's coast, there are concerns about the effects of **desalination** of seawater used to meet the growing demand.

South America

The Atacama is a narrow strip of desert running along nearly 620 miles (1,000 km) of Chile's coast, in the rain shadow of the Andes Mountains to the

east, with **prevailing** winds from the southeast. A cold current in the Pacific Ocean also stops moisture from reaching the desert from the west, although fog does occur. The Atacama is the driest desert on Earth.

Farther south, the Patagonian Desert also lies in the Andes' rain shadow, even though it lies on the opposite, eastern side of the mountains. Here the prevailing winds are from the northwest. The Patagonian Desert is in Argentina and is the largest desert in the Americas.

Southern Africa

Southern Africa's deserts are the Namib and the Kalahari. They lie close to each other but are distinctly different. The Namib is a narrow coastal strip, mostly located in Namibia. Created by a cold current that runs north from the Antarctic, it is about 1,180 miles (1,900 km) long and 100 miles (160 km) wide at its widest point. With only about one and a quarter inches (30 mm) of average annual rainfall, it is extremely arid. Coastal fog brings tiny amounts of much-needed moisture to the land and helps to support some specialized life-forms, including hardy grasses, dwarf shrubs, and **lichens**, as well as rodents such as gerbils, Grant's golden moles, and mole rats. About 70 species of lizards

Coastal Desert

The dry Atacama Desert in Chile, South America, meets the cold and wet Pacific Ocean, creating a sharp contrast between the two environments. The Atacama Desert stretches along the coast for more than 600 miles (1,000 km) but derives no benefit from this proximity in the form of extra rainfall. However, local coastal mists do provide a little moisture for hardy plants.

Kalahari Clouds

Clouds gathering in the sky above the Kalahari Desert in South Africa, promising much-needed precipitation. This desert is not as dry as some and, due to intermittent rainfall, has plenty of vegetation in parts of its huge expanse.

live in the desert, around 25 of which are found nowhere else on Earth. The desert's sand dunes are among the highest in the world, reaching up to 985 feet (300 m) tall. The Kalahari is far less dry and supports some rough scrub vegetation. It lies inland in Botswana, Namibia, and South Africa, covering large areas of high plateau and **salt flats**.

Northern Africa

Northern Africa's massive Sahara Desert covers almost 3.5 million square miles (9 million sq km)—8 percent of the world's land surface—and encompasses 16 countries, including Algeria, Sudan, Mali, Niger, Libya, and Chad. It continues all the way around the Horn of Africa and merges at its eastern end with the Arabian Desert. The Sahara varies greatly. It goes from sandy desert to mountains such as the Ahaggar range, from the fertile floodplains of the Nile and Niger Rivers to stony expanses below sea level. Much of the Sahara is extremely arid, with less than one inch (25 mm) of annual rainfall. Winds can be as strong as 62 miles

Desert Islands

The Canary Islands off the west coast of North Africa are part of the Sahara, although they are owned by Spain. Much of the area's economy relies on tourism. Thousands of people come every year from northern Europe in search of sun and warmth. This puts huge pressure on the limited resources of these islands. Water is of particular concern. All tourists expect high standards—swimming pools, golf courses, and constant running water in their rooms. All of these facilities use up water, and there is serious concern over just how long the region can cope with the demand.

(100 km) per hour. Desertification due to overgrazing and the felling of the area's few trees is occurring in the south (the Sahel region) and in Sudan and the Horn of Africa.

Crossing Deserts

Camel drivers resting in the sands of the desert with the world-famous pyramids of Giza in the background. This part of the North African country of Egypt is an eastern extension of the huge Sahara Desert.

Desert City

An aerial view of Dubai, a modern city in the United Arab Emirates on the Persian Gulf. Built in the desert, though not far from the coast, this city has grown into a major business and world tourist destination, complete with private islands and exclusive golf, yacht, and racing clubs for the super-rich to enjoy.

The Middle East

The Arabian Desert is an extension of the Sahara and encompasses the oil-rich nations of the Middle East, as well as Israel and Palestine. It includes the Empty Quarter, or Rub' al-Khali, the largest sand desert in the world at almost 230,000 square miles (600,000 sq km). Farther east, the Thar Desert lies to the east of the Indus River and straddles the Pakistani and Indian borders. Oil extraction in the Arabian Gulf brings many threats and problems to the desert, such as political instability, pollution, and the need to provide water for people.

Central Asia

The Turkestan, Takla Makan, and Gobi Deserts are central Asia's three continental deserts. All are very cold in the winter due to their northerly latitude and, in the case of the Takla Makan and Gobi, their high altitudes. The Turkestan Desert lies in a number of countries: Kazakstan, Uzbekistan, and Turkmenistan, as well as Russia. When under Soviet control, this desert saw one of the 20th century's greatest ecological disasters when two rivers that drain into the Aral Sea were diverted to irrigate cotton fields, causing the sea to shrink.

The Takla Makan lies in China and is widely regarded as the most inhospitable place on Earth, although people nonetheless regularly attempt to cross it for trading purposes. The Gobi desert lies in China and Mongolia and has one of the harshest winter temperatures of any desert region, due partly to the fact that it is so far from the warming influence of any sea or ocean.

Australia

Australia is an island continent, and more than three-quarters of it is desert, or "outback," as it is known in Australia. The Great Sandy, Great Victorian, and Gibson Deserts merge into what is known as the Western Desert. Here, mountain ranges contrast with sand dunes. Farther east in the country's interior is the low-lying Simpson Desert. Sheep grazing, farming, and mineral extraction are putting great pressure on the available water supply and are draining the Great Artesian Basin, an ancient aquifer that lies beneath the eastern side of the Simpson Desert.

Red Dunes

The huge, red sand dunes of the Simpson Desert in south-central Australia, the largest of which is known as the Big Red. Animals that have been introduced to this desert from other countries, such as the rabbit and the camel, cause many ecological problems for the native plants and animals.

Desert Life Under Threat

Some people may think that deserts are lifeless wastelands that are not particularly important or worth protecting. However, although desert life is not always very visible, deserts are home to many amazing plants and animals that have evolved there and nowhere else. There are about 1,200 species of plants in the Sahara Desert alone, for example. Lizards, snakes, rodents, bats, and birds all have made deserts their homes. About 13 percent of the world's human population lives in deserts as well.

Desert Plants: The Life That Supports Life

Plants are needed for other life to survive, providing food for animals and organic matter that helps make the soil life-sustaining. They also help to maintain soil, as their roots protect it from erosion. Plants need water to remain rigid and carry nutrients into their cells. Since water is so scarce in the desert, each plant's roots need to occupy a large area of land to extract the amount of water the plant needs to live. Therefore, on average, there are far fewer plants in the desert than in any other biome. Plants have evolved in many ways to cope with scarce water and the forms in which it appears in the desert—whether as a downpour, dew, fog, or mist, from deep underground, or in salt flats and marshes.

Some desert plants are short-lived, which can make them very vulnerable to changes in their environment. These plants bloom after a rain,

covering the desert briefly in bright and often large flowers as different species compete to attract the insects that pollinate them. The life cycle of these plants happens quickly to make the most of sudden rain. Their seeds **germinate** promptly, they flower, and then they quickly form new seeds—some in as few as eight days. These seeds can remain in a dry, **dormant** state for years until the next rainfall.

The roots of desert plants have lots of adaptations to maximize water intake, and some specialize in growing down to the **water table**. The roots of the tamarisk tree can reach down 165 feet (50 m) and can even tolerate salty water. Such plants often grow along dry riverbeds because there is likely to be groundwater available for them to make use of.

Other plants can hold moisture by storing it and not transpiring (losing water from their leaves and stems) when it is hot. These

Color in the Desert

A low-growing cactus in full bloom. These hardy plants have adapted to the dry conditions of deserts. They are what is known as succulent, which means they are able to store water for long periods of time in their stems. When rains finally come, the plants bloom and reproduce.

One of Earth's Oldest Living Things

Of the Namib Desert's unique plant species, Welwitschia mirabilis is truly amazing. According to carbon dating tests, it can live for about 2,000 years. It relies largely on fog from the Atlantic Ocean for water. The fog condenses onto its broad leaves and runs toward its long taproot. *With only two leaves—each split into strips and measuring more than six and a half feet (2 m) long—it is a primitive plant.*

plants are called **succulents** and **euphorbias**. A common succulent in American deserts is the cactus, the largest of which is the saguaro, which can grow to 60 feet tall (18 m) and live for more than 100 years. American desert succulents also include the spiny-leaved agaves, such as the Mexican century plant, thought to flower once a century although it actually flowers more often, and the yuccas. Euphorbias grow in Africa and other hot deserts.

Threats to Plants

Native desert species have come under threat from heavy grazing by goats and sheep and from intensive farming practices in countries such as Australia. One effect of removing native plants through grazing is that soil is exposed to the elements and becomes hard and baked by the sun. When rains arrive, they run off the surface and are wasted, instead of soaking into the soil where they can be stored in the water table.

Desert Animals—Survival Tactics

In order to survive in the desert, animals have several adaptations. Camels can go for miles without eating or drinking. They store food as fat in their humps, and they can drink a huge amount at once, allowing them to go weeks without drinking. They are perfectly adapted to withstand the desert extremes of hot and cold and are able to feed on tough desert plants. Related animals with similar adaptations are the llama, alpaca, and vicuna.

Wild herbivores that move far or fast include antelopes, gazelles, and Australia's kangaroo; all can travel to water and pastures and have strong teeth to chew tough leaves or grasses. Some deserts also feature fast carnivores—hyenas and cats, including lions in the Sahara and Kalahari, cheetahs in Africa and the Middle East, pumas or mountain lions in some American deserts and Africa and Asia, and caracals (a type of lynx) in Africa and India. Smaller carnivores feed on insects, arachnids, small reptiles, and herbivores. Deserts are home to many small herbivores, especially rodents; their small size helps them find shade, burrow into the

Traditional Desert Food Plants

Date palms are the best-known plants of the Arabian Desert, where they have been grown in **oases** *for more than 5,000 years. Each year, these tall palm trees can produce up to 100 pounds (45 kg) of dates—nutritious fruit that can be dried and kept. Dates are the most important* **cash crop** *in many Saharan oases. Fig and almond trees from the Middle East are now grown more widely (including in the U.S.). In the Americas, traditional food plants include quinoa, which originates in the Andes Mountains and produces seeds that are very high in protein. There is now increasing interest in growing traditional food plants such as quinoa commercially in semiarid areas since they require little water.*

Food from Oases

A grove of date palms at an oasis in Tunisia, in North Africa. Harvested dates, with their high energy content, have been a staple food of desert peoples for thousands of years.

Desert Rodents

Many small rodents have adapted to the hard life of the desert. This Cape ground squirrel uses its tail to shield itself from the sun. It is found in the deserts of southern Africa.

Shrinking Water Tables

*Water tables sit beneath the surface of the land and act as natural **reservoirs** of water. They feed the landscape with water when there is no rain and rivers on the surface dry up. They are vital to the health of dry regions around the world. However, they are under serious threat. As the human population grows and our standards of living develop, we need increased amounts of water, much of which we get from the water table, causing it to shrink. In China, for example, it is estimated that the water table is shrinking at a rate of three feet (0.9 m) per year.*

Desert Mammals

A male lion prowling the dry bed of the Nossob River in Namibia. Large mammals cope with the heat of the desert by moving around as little as possible during the day, although in general they are not well-suited to this biome.

sand to escape the heat, and find food. Rodents' teeth are always growing, which helps them eat tough plants.

Many desert animals have been hunted for years and are now rare. Poaching in parts of Africa for antelope hides and horns, for instance, has drastically reduced large herds. Other animals

have lost their already scarce plant food due to overgrazing by domesticated animals. A number of nature reserves have been set up in the past 30 years to help reverse these trends.

Desert Reptiles

An Agama lizard of South Africa basks in the heat of the desert sun. These cold-blooded animals are ideally adapted to the conditions of their desert environments.

Controlling Body Temperature

Controlling body temperature is hard in the desert. Mammals seek out shade in the daytime sun, and many burrow into the sand. Some, such as the Mojave ground squirrel, become dormant during hot periods, a technique called estivation. Many others hide away in the daytime, an adaptation called diurnation. Reptiles are cold-blooded animals and do not create their own internal heat. In the desert, they regulate their temperature by basking in the sun to warm up and burrowing in the sand to cool down. An animal's behavior can also help; some lizards do "thermal dancing," lifting their feet to keep them from getting hot.

A Plague of Locusts

Locusts are desert insects—a group of about 12 related grasshoppers. They occasionally become active after heavy rains and turn from solitary into swarm animals, although scientists do not know for certain exactly what triggers their swarming instincts. They travel huge distances, devastating vast areas of vegetation by eating them bare. The largest recorded swarm was estimated to consist of 40 billion individual locusts!

Desert Insects

The desert locust has adapted to desert life and can eat any plant material available. When locusts swarm, they can devastate farmers' crops in a matter of minutes.

Nomads

To survive in desert conditions, people have developed special lifestyles. Supplies of water and food are the most crucial requirements, and a **nomadic** way of life is the one best suited to desert conditions. There are different forms of nomadism. The Australian Aborigines practiced it to hunt and gather food as they moved between water holes. In other parts of the world, desert nomads were pastoralists, keeping a herd of camels, sheep, or goats, which provided food, milk, and wool or hides to make rugs, clothing, and temporary homes. Seminomads spend some of the year settled in villages while planting and harvesting crops.

These various forms of nomadism mean a **sustainable** and respectful presence within the environment. This way of life is by necessity simple: belongings are pared down to enable pack animals to carry them. It is a **subsistence** lifestyle, in which people produce what they need and barter for things they cannot produce. Today, this simple lifestyle is under enormous threat. Many governments prefer for land to be divided and owned by people or companies, as this makes it easier to control and tax. Borders between countries may be hard to cross; the Sahara spreads across 16 countries, many of which face serious political instability and civil war. Nomads cannot compete for water when it is extracted or dammed for use in commercial agriculture or by companies to support industrial mining plants.

In many parts of the world, governments are pushing nomadic peoples to settle down, as they are often seen as troublesome and on the margins of regulated society. A recent example of this is the Bushmen of the Kalahari Desert, who are being moved away from their traditional homes to make way for oil exploration. Once moved, such nomadic people lose their independence and often their self-respect.

Oases and Settled Life

For thousands of years, deserts have provided people with land on which to develop settled communities, provided that water can be obtained from some reliable source or other. Settlements

Desert Life Today

A modern desert-dweller, this Bedouin leads the traditional animal of the desert, the camel, with a herd of sheep in the background, while talking on a cell phone.

can be as small as an oasis where natural spring water feeds simple irrigation systems that support a few date palms, which give shade to more delicate fruit trees and vegetables. Or, they can be as large as cities, such as Cairo in Egypt, that have grown up around complex and large-scale irrigation systems on the banks of major rivers.

The planning, management, and maintenance of irrigation systems requires thoughtful social organization. These systems need to be devised and built collectively, and water use needs to be agreed upon. The Tigris and Euphrates Rivers, which gave rise to Mesopotamia (modern-day Iraq), the Nile River in Egypt, the Amu Darya (Oxus River) and Syr Darya in central Asia, the Indus in what is now Pakistan, and China's Yellow River (Huang He) are all examples of major rivers that enabled civilizations to flourish on a large scale, providing the area with a reliable and plentiful supply of life-giving water.

Small-scale oasis life still goes on: there are very productive oases throughout the Sahara, Middle Eastern deserts, and farther east. Many different forms of irrigation have been developed. For example, in Iran, the ancient qanat system is still employed. It involves constructing underground galleries to carry water from nearby aquifers at higher altitudes down to the crops growing on the plains. Water is guided down to the plants with very little loss from evaporation.

When Irrigation Goes Wrong

Throughout the centuries, some civilizations based on irrigation have gradually fallen to ruin. Some perhaps began to take their surroundings for granted, and irrigation degraded the soil by allowing salination to occur. Salination occurs when too much salt accumulates on land over time as it is deposited by irrigation water. This happened in Mesopotamia, where by 1700 B.C., crop yields had begun to drop dramatically. It is likely, too, that climate change has come into play, making areas drier than they once were and more prone to droughts. This probably affected the

Pueblo Peoples

Pueblo, Spanish for "village," is a name given to different Native American peoples who have lived in the deserts of New Mexico and Arizona for many centuries, building villages on or close to mesas. They are thought to be descended from or related to the Anasazi, who, from about the 11th to 14th centuries, flourished in areas such as what is now Mesa Verde National Park in southwestern Colorado. Today, this park gives visitors an opportunity to visit a few of its more than 1,000 archaeological sites. These sites consist of groups of fragile cliff dwellings dug out of the soft sandstone. Later Native American peoples, such as the Hopi, found that these arid areas could support an agricultural civilization with a dense population, based on careful management and irrigation.

Pueblo Homes

Cliff dwellings of the ancient Pueblo Indians of the Mesa Verde in southwest Colorado, dating from the 11th to 14th centuries.

Fertile Crescent, an area of the Middle East that was once fertile and supported large numbers of people but is now desert.

Major Disasters

In the 20th century, some spectacular disasters demonstrated the need to develop irrigation systems carefully and treat the desert biome with care. Two examples make this point vividly: the Aral Sea and Salton Lake.

The Aral Sea is really an inland salt lake, the fourth-largest in the world. It is fed by two rivers, the Amu Darya and Syr Darya, that flow down from mountains in central Asia. In the 1960s, the Soviet government created cotton fields in previously uncultivated areas, increasing the amount of irrigation in the area to water these crops by diverting the rivers. The Aral Sea shrank to half its size and became very salty, killing the fish and putting an end to the local fishing industry. It also brought local climate change; since there was less evaporated moisture in the air, the winters became colder and drier. Dust storms also carried highly polluting salts from the dried lake.

In the U.S., a polluted lake was created in the early 1900s when, as part of an irrigation plan, people tried to divert part of the Colorado River. This enormously important river flows through a massive area of deserts, and its tributaries provide the main source of water for these areas. The irrigation plan failed, and the Colorado poured into a salty depression called the Salton Trough, turning this dry land into a lake. The river flow was brought under control, but the lake created by this disaster is still polluted.

Salty Sea

The polluted Salton Sea is a very salty environment and—at 376 square miles (974 sq km)—the largest inland lake in California.

Desertification

The United Nations Convention to Combat Desertification (UNCCD) has developed a working definition of desertification: "land degradation in arid, semiarid, and sub-humid areas resulting from various factors, including climatic variations and human activities." This sums up what most experts agree on—that people are involved in causing desertification. "Desert" is what we call the healthy natural biome. An area suffering from desertification is not a desert in that positive sense, but degraded land that has lost its natural fertility. A widely held misconception is that desertification is when desert sand dunes encroach onto agricultural and lived-in areas. In most cases, this is untrue. Desertification is a gradual and complicated process that can happen anywhere. It has happened in parts of Spain and on America's Great Plains, for example.

Why Does Desertification Matter?

Experts estimate that desertification affects an area approximately the size of Brazil and that close to one-third of Earth's land surface is under threat of future desertification. Desertification can spell famine for some populations, especially in less developed countries; people cannot grow food on affected areas, which can lead to poverty and famine if there are no food reserves. This leads to an increase in economic migrants—people forced to move elsewhere to try to provide for themselves.

The Causes of Desertification

Desertification usually involves human actions and may also be affected by climate change. Evidence shows that climate change happens naturally in desert areas over many thousands of years. This is likely reinforced by human-induced climate change, which means major droughts may be linked to the **greenhouse effect**.

People have been causing desertification for thousands of years by cutting down trees and shrubs to burn for fuel, clearing land for agriculture, allowing animals to overgraze, and planting single crops in unsuitable areas. In more recent times, modern medicine has also had an impact. In the 1970s and early 1980s, the Sahel region of the Sahara experienced catastrophic droughts. At the time, the area had among the highest birth rates in the world, which put heavy pressure on the land.

The effects of modern medicine also tie in to overgrazing. Traditionally, nomads eat the meat from their animals only occasionally, to mark festive times. Today, with better veterinary care, herds can grow larger, and as more people become city dwellers, there is a ready market for meat. As a result, pastoralists keep larger herds to benefit from this opportunity. This puts greater pressures on the available pastures and is unsustainable: it eventually causes desertification as the animals eat the available vegetation, which then cannot regenerate.

What Are the Solutions?

In the 20th century, people recognized that they needed to take action to stop desertification. Since the 1930s, scientists have been carrying out research and publishing reports on this problem. The Sahel region's droughts of the 1970s and '80s, as well as dramatic television news coverage that showed starving people and animals, prompted the United Nations to call an International Conference on Desertification in 1977, which was attended by representatives of nearly 100 countries and governmental and nongovernmental organizations from around the world. By 1996, the UNCCD was established.

Today, many organizations are devoted to combating desertification, but there is no single solution. At an international level, fighting the greenhouse effect that contributes to **global warming** and climate change and reducing all forms of pollution are crucial for the health of all biomes. At a local level, there needs to be a realistic approach to just how much the land can produce in terms of crops and support in terms of animal numbers.

Many debates remain, however. Developed and developing countries often disagree on key issues, such as quotas for the emission of **greenhouse gases.** The pressures on less

Desert Dump
An abandoned car in scrub land close to Cape Town, South Africa, stands as a symbol of the lack of care and understanding that many people show toward desert regions.

economically developed countries to generate income—by producing cash crops, for instance—are also hard to resist, especially when countries have debts to pay to the **World Bank**. Additionally, many farmers face pressure to take short-term measures to provide for their families. All of this can easily outweigh the need to nurture the land for the longer term.

Increasingly, people feel that solutions need to be appropriate to their particular area. For example, in Niger, one of the Sahel countries affected by drought, many people now believe it is wrong to cut down native trees and scrub to increase cultivated land. The natural vegetation forms a valuable "green belt" on desert margins and around smaller, more sustainable agricultural land. This provides protection from winds and consists of many native plant species that can withstand local conditions.

Overall, the key to fighting desertification is to ensure that the environment is treated with respect, so that native life-forms can flourish, as they are what guarantee its health. People also

Desert Fences

This man is planting a straw fence designed to capture the shifting sands of the Gobi Desert and help prevent desertification on the eastern border of China.

The Dust Bowl

*The "Dust Bowl" is the name given to an ecological disaster that happened in the 1930s when, during a period of drought, a vast area of the Great Plains in the U.S. suffered massive wind erosion, with much of the topsoil being blown away from once fertile soils in Kansas, Colorado, Oklahoma, and Texas. This occurred because vast areas of **monoculture** were being subjected to poor farming practices that made them vulnerable. Plains grassland had been turned over to wheat fields, and constant deep plowing exposed the soil. The resulting tragedy showed that desertification affects not only less economically developed countries, such as those of the Sahel, but also wealthy nations.*

Wind Erosion

This photograph taken in the 1930s in midwestern America, the region known as the Dust Bowl, graphically captures the effects of wind eroding and blowing away fragile topsoil from farmland.

need to think beyond short-term gain. Irrigation systems need to be sustainable and not draw on water that cannot be replaced; otherwise, the water table is altered and natural vegetation cannot survive. People must grow each year's crop as they maintain the long-term health of the environment.

Today's Changing Deserts

With an ever-growing population and technology so sophisticated that we can aspire to visit Mars, it is not surprising that we are starting to populate deserts—often called the "final frontier" because they offer the last land available for colonizing. Since the earliest civilizations, people have moved away from lands that they outgrew or exhausted. Within a short time of colonizing new lands, such as the Americas and Australia in the 1700s and 1800s, people often found that their impact had spoiled these areas. In the 21st century, efforts are being made to inhabit deserts in a respectful way. However, economic pressures are also very real, and the challenge remains to balance these conflicting needs.

The main pressures people place on the desert biome are caused by the various economic activities they pursue there. These pertain to agriculture and grazing, mineral extraction and mining, space and military research, and tourism. All of these activities require energy and water, as well as the infrastructure of everyday life for the people involved in the work. Indeed, settlements in deserts are now causing a relatively new pressure. Not only are people living in deserts to complete the various work done there; now, more tourists are visiting deserts, and more people are choosing to retire and live there.

Glen Canyon Dam

Glen Canyon Dam on the Colorado River near Page, Arizona, was built in 1955 to create a reservoir (Lake Powell) to supply water for homes and industry in the region.

Agriculture and Grazing

In places such as the North African oases and the Nile **delta** in Egypt, desert land has been put to agricultural use for thousands of years. Today, far more produce is grown for export than ever before, and it is supported by high technology. Egypt provides all kinds of fresh vegetables, as well as cash crops such as rice and cotton, to local and European markets. Its reliance on the Nile has changed dramatically since the building of the Aswan High Dam in the second half of the 20th century. Irrigation now takes place throughout the year, as the Nile no longer floods, and people grow two crops a year instead of one.

Modern-day agricultural practices are varied in arid or semiarid environments. High-technology irrigation solutions are expensive and cannot be developed in countries that don't have another major source of wealth. In Saudi Arabia, funds are available from the oil industry to provide sophisticated, electronically controlled irrigation systems called rotating sprinklers that make very effective use of water.

In poorer areas, **intermediate technology** is used to adapt traditional irrigation systems and minimize water loss through evaporation or other negative effects.

Fertile Nile

For thousands of years, the seasonal flooding of the Nile River in Sudan has supplied people farming on the banks of the river with fertile soils.

Fossil Fuels and Mineral Extraction

Because many desert areas are rich in fossil fuels and minerals, people are attracted to these inhospitable places in pursuit of wealth. In Australia's deserts, valuable minerals such as gold, opals, and various metal ores are found. Namibia has diamonds and many other minerals. Tunisia has Africa's largest reserves of phosphate, used in fertilizer. Mexico has the most mineral reserves of any desert country and is the largest producer of silver.

Mining can have a major impact on the landscape and environment, due to the numbers of people involved in operations and the environmental effects of the mining itself. Australia's outback today has many ghost towns and abandoned mines where mining fell out of favor. Sometimes people discovered mines where the minerals were easier to extract, and other times one mined ore was replaced by a more desirable one.

Desert Economy

Deserts can be of economic importance to people due to the minerals and fossil fuels that may be found in them. These men work at a mining plant in South Africa.

Desert Oil

Oil fields in the desert of Kuwait, a country in the Middle East. Kuwait produces about 700 million barrels of oil a year, which brings in about 75 percent of the country's income.

Oil

A large proportion of the world's oil and natural gas comes from desert countries, including the U.S., Algeria, and Libya. About half of the world's oil reserves are believed to be in the Middle East. The Gulf States are very rich in oil, and they are 100 percent arid. Traditionally, a tiny population of nomadic herdspeople lived in the desert, with small trading and fishing ports on the coasts, where products from oases and pearl diving were sold. Now these countries get their wealth from fossil fuels. They are very rich and can afford to pay for what they need to support the oil and gas industry—building desalination plants for drinking water, for example. But possessing such riches poses problems other than the difficulties of oil extraction in an arid environment. It can also cause political instability. Kuwait, a tiny country with the world's largest oil reserves, was invaded by Iraq in 1991, causing the first Gulf War. Oil-rich countries need to diversify to ensure political stability in the future, as war is a major threat to the health of the desert biome and the people who live in and around it.

Tourism, Retirement, and Water Issues

Tourism is a growing resource for desert areas, especially in the U.S. Canyons and rock features provide ideal locations for outdoor pursuits, such as hiking, rock climbing, and camping. In deserts with archaeological riches, tourism is also a major resource. Egypt is a prime example, with its ancient heritage providing the basis for a booming tourist industry.

The climate of some deserts is itself a major attraction. Many tourists appreciate the dry and sunny climate, especially in places where desert and sea go hand in hand, such as in the Canary Islands or on the coasts of Morocco and Tunisia. The desert climate also attracts growing numbers of Americans to retire in the American Southwest. Popular desert cities include Phoenix, Arizona, and Las Vegas, Nevada, which are really oasis cities dependent on the Colorado River for their water. Today, the sustainability of population growth in this area is under question.

Water in Desert Cities

An aerial photograph of Las Vegas, Nevada. The presence of all the people who live in this desert city puts an enormous strain on the water resources of the region.

Space Telescope

The Hubble Space Telescope, *named after astronomer Edwin Hubble, was launched into space in 1990.*

Space, Defense, and High-Tech Industries

Since open land is hard to obtain in so many parts of the world, it is hardly surprising that deserts have attracted industrialists, scientists, and people in defense-related industries in which there is a need for room to carry out experiments or test equipment—and where it is also important to keep prying eyes at a distance. Military nuclear research has been carried out in deserts in the former Soviet Union, the U.S., and Australia, leaving vast areas contaminated. For example, Maralinga in South Australia was home to one of Great Britain's major nuclear testing sites in the 1950s and '60s. Disputes continue today over contamination in the area and its effects on the people there.

Space researchers are attracted to deserts because of the low levels of light pollution and clear skies that go with the dry climate. For example, the Mount Wilson Observatory, made famous by the work of Edwin Hubble, who worked there in the 1920s, lies in the desert in California. Chile's Atacama Desert, meanwhile, is home to the world's second-largest telescope. Many high-tech industries today are attracted to desert areas in the U.S., largely because the means are available to tame the hot climate with air-conditioning and other modern comforts, and the atmosphere is relatively unpolluted and sterile.

The Sunbelt States

Arizona, Colorado, Nevada, New Mexico, and Utah are the U.S. states with the greatest population growth today. All rely largely on the Colorado River and its tributaries for their water. They make up one of the most economically developed desert areas in the world, complete with mining, cattle ranching, agriculture, tourism, and high-tech industries. People's standard of living is high: about half of the homes in Phoenix have a swimming pool. In the late 1920s, the Hoover Dam was built on the border of Nevada and Arizona, creating a major reservoir called Lake Mead. Since then, major dams, reservoirs, and hydroelectric plants have been built. Experts believe that they cannot rely on the Colorado to supply all of the population's needs, so desalination and other measures are being explored to increase water supplies. There also are growing tensions between different interest groups that want their share of water. Mexico and the U.S. are sometimes at odds, as the Colorado flows through both countries. Farmers and the authorities that regulate water use clash as well, as do Native Americans and the same authorities.

Desalination

With fresh water in high demand, there are thousands of desalination plants around the world. These are factories where salt is removed from seawater. There are various ways to do this, and all are costly. Distillation is one method. Through the distillation process, water is evaporated, separating into water vapor and various salts and trace minerals. The vapor is then condensed into fresh water. Most desalination occurs in wealthy desert countries, such as the oil-rich nations of the Middle East.

Scientists hope to soon develop practical ways to use solar energy to power desalination plants, but even with clean and renewable energy resources, there are issues over what to do with the salt-rich water that is left over. In the American Southwest, there are ongoing discussions about discharging such by-products into the Gulf of California or the Pacific Ocean.

The Future of Deserts

Today, governments and groups around the world are working to protect the desert biome. If people learn to live in and use the desert biome in a sustainable way, they can avoid having a negative effect on the environment. By carefully preserving the desert's delicate natural balance, people can benefit from its resources without destroying its beauty in the process.

New Forms of Income

One of the main reasons many countries and peoples exploit deserts is to make a profit. In order to encourage people to protect valuable desert landscapes, new ways in which desert areas can create economic value are being explored. For example, eco-tourism is being developed in many deserts so that people can visit oases and remote desert areas in a manner that does the least amount of damage to the environment, while also bringing tourist dollars to the region. Another way of bringing income into environmentally sensitive areas without damaging them is to utilize the trade of traditional goods, such as textiles. Many nomadic and seminomadic peoples have created hand-made carpets and rugs from their animals' wool for hundreds of years. Jewelry made with local minerals and metals is also sold in many desert areas. These are often high-value items.

National Parks

Countries such as the U.S. have made several desert areas into national parks, which have strict rules about access to ensure that breeding birds or rare species are carefully protected. They also limit visitor numbers and set clear standards about respectful behavior, forbidding littering, plant picking, and polluting. The parks create limited employment for local people and generate income through entry fees, which can be reinvested to help safeguard the environment.

Desert Monuments

A woman viewing the Mitten buttes in Monument Valley Tribal Park. This famous valley, where many Western movies were filmed, is now protected Navajo land on the border of Arizona and Utah.

Conservation Organizations

There are many organizations, both national and international, that monitor life in fragile and endangered habitats around the world, including deserts. They help to ensure that these environments will survive long into the future. Here are some of the more well-known ones:

- **Friends of the Earth**   www.foe.org
Founded in 1971 in Britain, Friends of the Earth is now one of the world's best-known and most respected environmental pressure groups.
- **World Wide Fund for Nature (WWF)**   www.panda.org
Founded in 1961, this Swiss-based organization raises money to fund conservation operations around the world, focusing in particular on endangered animals.
- **Greenpeace**   www.greenpeace.org/usa/
Founded in 1971 in Canada, Greenpeace has grown to become one of the world's biggest and most influential environmental pressure groups. It campaigns all over the world on behalf of the environment.
- **International Union for the Conservation of Nature (IUCN)**   www.iucn.org
This organization publishes books listing all of the world's endangered animals and habitats. These books present the most comprehensive picture we have of the state of the planet in terms of threats to species.

What You Can Do to Help

You are part of the future. This is your world as much as it is anyone else's. Helping protect deserts that may be far away might not seem terribly important, but they need our help as much as the rain forests, the oceans, and all of the other great biomes that make up our amazing living planet. There are plenty of ways in which we can all help make the world a safe and lasting place for the animals and plants that live with us. Here are a few ways you might help desert biomes:

- Be careful in selecting plants for your garden or as presents. Some desert plants are very rare, and taking them from their natural setting to make a profit harms the environment. In some countries, it is illegal to sell rare plants.
- Get involved in efforts to raise people's awareness of the fragility of natural desert environments through projects at school or with local clubs.
- Find out more at school about the fascinating lives of desert animals and the weird and wonderful plants that have evolved to survive in this environment.

- Support one or more of the many organizations dedicated to protecting deserts. Fund-raising events and awareness days often feature fun activities.
- If you are lucky enough to live close to a desert or are able to travel to one, make a photograph presentation to explain to friends and family why the environment should be treated with respect.
- Always use water wisely, especially in a desert environment.
- Have respect for the people who live in desert regions.
- Remember, whatever delicate and beautiful natural environment you find yourself in, take nothing but photographs and leave nothing but footprints. That way, you will always leave wild places in the same state in which you found them.

Further Reading

Allaby, Michael. *Biomes Atlases: Deserts and Semideserts*. Austin, Tex.: Raintree, 2003.

Johnson, Rebecca. *A Walk in the Desert*. Minneapolis: Carolrhoda Books, 2001.

MacQuitty, Miranda. *Desert*. New York: Dorling Kindersley, 2000.

Martin, Michael. *Deserts of the Earth*. New York: Thames & Hudson, 2004.

Ricciuti, Edward. *Desert*. New York: Benchmark Books, 1996.

Riley, Peter. *Survivor's Science in the Desert*. Chicago: Raintree, 2005.

Web sites

A Day in the Desert

http://gorp.away.com/gorp/publishers/wildernesspress/hik_desert0.htm

Cold Deserts of the World

http://mbgnet.mobot.org/sets/desert/cold.htm

The Desert Biome

http://www.ucmp.berkeley.edu/glossary/gloss5/biome/deserts.html

Deserts: Geology and Resources

http://pubs.usgs.gov/gip/deserts

Desert Survival

http://www.ci.phoenix.az.us/FIRE/desert.html

DesertUSA

http://www.desertusa.com

Glossary

Cash crop   A crop, such as coffee or cotton, grown for sale and not for use by the farmer or community that grew it.

Deforestation   The removal of forests and woodlands, usually by people. Reasons include clearing land for agriculture or industry and timber harvesting.

Delta   A triangular deposit of soil at the mouth of a river.

Desalination   The process by which salt is taken out of seawater so that it can be used for drinking or watering crops.

Desertification   Human actions that turn fertile land into sterile desert, through overgrazing, loss of vegetation, and soil erosion.

Dormant   A state in which an organism shuts down its energy use to a bare minimum in order to survive during difficult periods, such as winter or times of drought.

Ecological   Relating to the study of living organisms and their relationships with the environment.

Ecosystems   Natural units of the environment in which all of the plants, animals, and nonliving components depend on each other in complex ways.

Eco-tourism   Tourism based upon a more sensitive approach to the impact that travelers have upon the landscapes they visit.

Euphorbias   Plants that have adapted to growing and reproducing in hot, dry environments.

Evaporation   When water is heated and turns into vapor, it is said to have evaporated. Evaporation is part of the water cycle.

Evolved   Scientists believe that life on Earth has developed, or evolved, over billions of years. The theory of evolution claims that all life has come from single-celled forms and has slowly become more complex.

Germinate   The process of seeds becoming a plant. They are stimulated into growth by light, water, and food.

Global warming   The process by which Earth's climate is thought to be getting warmer through an increase in greenhouse gases.

Greenhouse effect   The greenhouse effect occurs when greenhouse gases act as a blanket in the atmosphere, trapping heat. People have added to these gases, and scientists fear this has warmed the global climate.

Greenhouse gases   Gases, including carbon dioxide and methane, that trap heat in Earth's atmosphere.

Habitats   Parts of an environment that are self-contained, supplying the needs of the organisms that live within them.

Hydroelectric plants   Plants where electricity is produced by using the force and energy from moving water, such as a large river that has been dammed.

Intermediate technology   The use of technology and engineering inventions made in developed, industrial countries but applied to the needs of poorer, Third World nations.

Irrigate   To take water from natural rivers, lakes, and rainfall to use on crops—for example, by building special channels along which the water can flow into fields.

Lichens   Life-forms that consist of a specific fungus and alga combined together. They grow on rocks and trees and can survive harsh conditions.

Mesas   Hills shaped like tables. They are found in eroded desert landscapes.

Monoculture   Growing just one crop to the exclusion of all other things, usually over a large area. This practice disrupts the natural life of the animals and other plants in the area.

Nomadic   A term that describes a wandering way of life. Nomadic people traditionally keep animals or follow the migratory paths of wild animals, living off the land and settling only for short periods of time.

Oases   Areas where water is found in an otherwise desert landscape. Oases are small, fertile places where animals, plants, and people live. (The singular form is oasis.)

Prevailing winds   A term used to describe the direction from which the winds most commonly blow in a region.

Reservoirs   Places where water collects and is stored. Usually the word is used of an artificial lake built by people to provide towns and cities with a constant and regular supply of water.

Salt flats   Areas of flat land covered in a surface layer of salt, formed as salty water evaporates in the heat of a desert.

Silt   Fine-grained sediment that is deposited by a river as it reaches flatter ground on its journey to the sea.

Subsistence   Living in a situation in which one has the bare means to survive—food, water, and shelter—but no surplus to trade.

Succulents   Plants that are able to hold lots of water in their stems and leaves, which makes them able to survive dry conditions.

Sustainable   Something that can be carried out indefinitely into the future.

Taproot   A long, single root in a plant that grows vertically downward. One example is the carrot.

Temperate   A term used to describe a climate that is neither too hot nor too cold. Temperate zones are found halfway between the hot tropics and the cold poles.

Tundra   Land close to or inside the Arctic Circle, where the layer of soil just below the surface is permanently frozen due to year-round low temperatures.

Water table   Beneath the ground, rainwater collects in the rocks. The depth at which these rocks are permanently wet is called the water table, and it generally follows the shape of the land above it.

World Bank   A special bank set up in 1945 after World War II to help restore the economies of the devastated countries. It is part of the United Nations.

Index